NEW YORK GIANTS

ALL-TIME GREATS

BY TED COLEMAN

Book design by Jake Slavik
Cover design by Jake Slavik

Photographs ©: Adam Hunger/AP Images, cover (top), 1 (top); Tony Tomsic/AP Images, cover (bottom), 1 (bottom); Pro Football Hall of Fame/AP Images, 4; John Lindsay/AP Images, 6; David Durochik/AP Images, 8; AP Images, 10; Al Messerschmidt/AP Images, 12, 16; Kathy Kmonicek/AP Images, 14; Stephen J. Boitano/AP Images, 18; Jerry Lai/AP Images, 19; Alika Jenner/AP Images, 21

Press Box Books, an imprint of Press Room Editions.

ISBN
978-1-63494-362-8 (library bound)
978-1-63494-379-6 (paperback)
978-1-63494-412-0 (epub)
978-1-63494-396-3 (hosted ebook)

Library of Congress Control Number: 2020952634

Distributed by North Star Editions, Inc.
2297 Waters Drive
Mendota Heights, MN 55120
www.northstareditions.com

Printed in the United States of America
082021

ABOUT THE AUTHOR

Ted Coleman is a sportswriter who lives in Louisville, Kentucky, with his trusty Affenpinscher, Chloe.

TABLE OF CONTENTS

FLAHERTY
1

CHAPTER 1

THE EARLY YEARS

The New York Giants have had many great players in their long history. End **Ray Flaherty** was so good that the team decided nobody else should ever wear the same uniform number. The team retired No. 1 after Flaherty left in 1935. Soon, other football teams followed suit to honor their greatest players.

Steve Owen started making a name for himself at tackle. Then he became a coaching legend for the Giants. Owen became the team's head coach in 1930 while he was still playing. He coached for 24 years and won two National Football League (NFL) titles.

In college, people called **Mel Hein** "Old Indestructible." Hein played both offense and defense for the Giants. He excelled as a center on offense and a tough linebacker on defense. Hein was named Most Valuable Player (MVP) of the NFL in 1938. He rarely missed a play during his 15-year career.

WELLINGTON MARA

Giants founder **Tim Mara** allowed his son **Wellington Mara** to be a ball boy in the 1925 season. Wellington worked with the Giants for the next 80 years. He became the team's main owner in 1959. Wellington was a huge figure in NFL history. His nickname, "The Duke," appears on every NFL football to this day.

Ken Strong also rarely left the field. He could do it all. Strong mainly played running back. But he also received, passed, kicked, and even played defense for the Giants. In the 1934 NFL title game, Strong racked up 17 points. He scored two touchdowns and kicked two extra points and a field goal.

STAT SPOTLIGHT

CAREER COACHING WINS

GIANTS TEAM RECORD

Steve Owen: 153

TUNNELL
45

CHAPTER 2

BUILDING BIG BLUE

In 1948, defensive back **Emlen Tunnell** became the first Black player in Giants history. He hitchhiked to New York City to ask for a tryout. Tunnell didn't just make the team. He set the NFL record for career interceptions. Tunnell also returned punts and set records for that, too.

By the time he retired in 1961, quarterback **Charlie Conerly** held most of the Giants' passing records. Conerly also led the team to one of its most famous victories. The Giants routed the mighty Chicago Bears 47–7 during the 1956 NFL Championship Game.

Conerly helped make the Giants one of the league's most popular teams.

Running back **Frank Gifford** earned MVP honors in 1956. He was still in the prime of his career during the 1960 season. But that year, he got knocked out of a game against the

Philadelphia Eagles. His head injury sidelined Gifford for 18 months. He returned in 1962 as a receiver. Gifford won Comeback Player of the Year.

Y. A. TITTLE

Quarterback **Y. A. Tittle** played just four seasons for the Giants. He was already 34 years old when he arrived. But Tittle showed he had plenty left. He earned MVP honors in 1963 and led the league in touchdowns twice. He failed to win a title, but he led some of the best Giants teams in history.

Left tackle **Rosey Brown** blocked for players such as Gifford. Brown was big, tough, and an expert at his job. He was also reliable. Brown missed only four games in 13 seasons. He went on to work for the Giants until his death in 2004.

STAT SPOTLIGHT

CAREER TOUCHDOWNS

GIANTS TEAM RECORD

Frank Gifford: 78

CARSON
53
GIANTS

CHAPTER 3

BIG BLUE WRECKING CREW

The Giants defense of the 1980s was something special. It was known as the "Big Blue Wrecking Crew." Linebacker **Harry Carson** came to the Giants in 1976. Big Blue managed to win only three games that year. But in the 1986 season, they became Super Bowl champs. Carson, a ferocious tackler, was a huge reason why.

Carson was joined by other legendary linebackers. The greatest was **Lawrence Taylor**. Taylor arrived in 1981. He was named NFL Defensive Player of the Year that season.

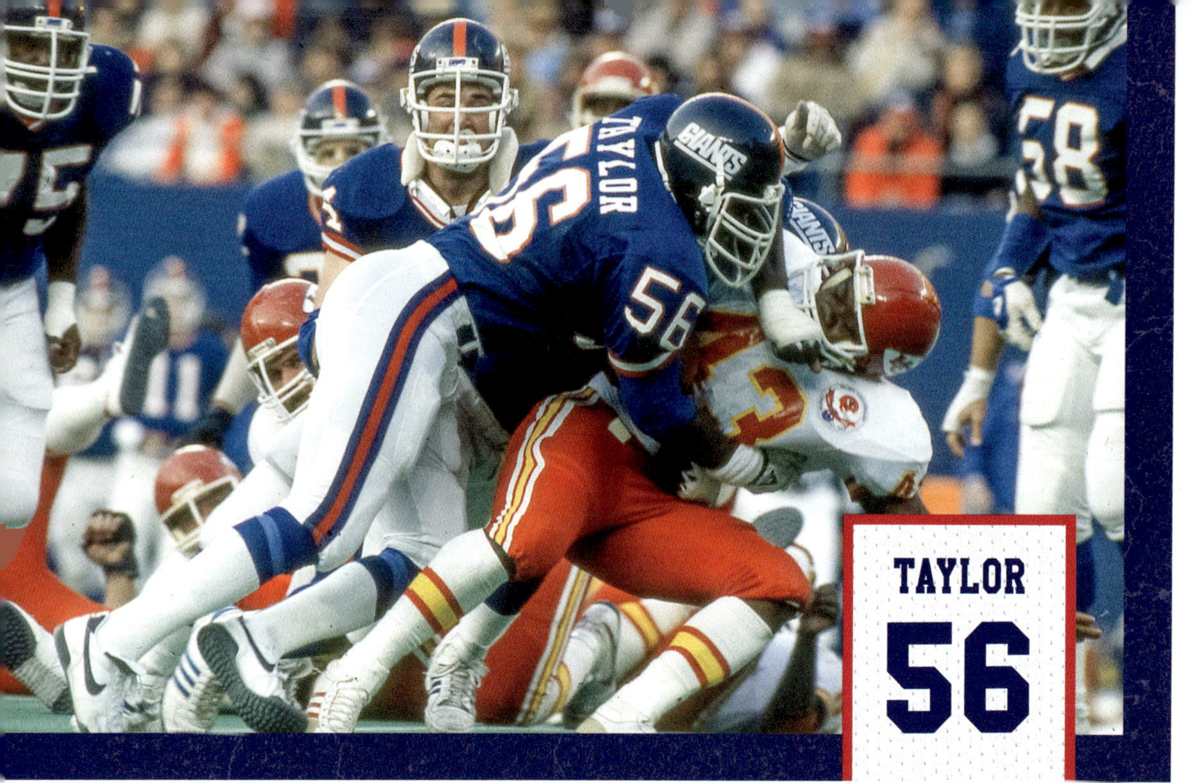

Taylor went on to win the award two more times. When he retired after the 1993 season, he had two Super Bowl rings. Taylor was among the top defensive players in NFL history.

Linebacker **Carl Banks** was the third overall pick in the 1984 draft. He became a key part of the Giants defense, winning two Super Bowl rings. In Super Bowl XXI, Banks recorded 14 tackles.

BILL PARCELLS

Bill Parcells was known as a defensive coach. He worked as the Giants' defensive coordinator before becoming head coach in 1983. He helped the Giants build one of the best defenses of the 1980s. He also led the team to two Super Bowls. Parcells retired for health reasons after the second title, but he returned later to coach other teams.

Big Blue was not all about defense, though. They had a great quarterback in **Phil Simms**. The Giants had struggled to find a franchise quarterback since the days of Charlie Conerly. Simms broke many of Conerly's records. He was rarely the best quarterback in the league. But he was great when it mattered most. Simms was the MVP of Super Bowl XXI.

STAT SPOTLIGHT

PASSING YARDS IN A GAME

GIANTS TEAM RECORD

Phil Simms: 513 (October 13, 1985)

STRAHAN
92

CHAPTER 4

NEXT SUPER BOWL ERA

The core of the Big Blue Wrecking Crew was gone by 1993. But two new players helped usher in a new era of Giants defense. Defensive end **Michael Strahan** struggled during his first few years. Then, in 1997, he broke out with 14.5 sacks. He made his first of seven Pro Bowls that year. He also helped lead the Giants back to Super Bowl glory in the 2007 season.

Linebacker **Jessie Armstead** also arrived in 1993. No one expected much of Armstead at first. After all, he was the 207th pick in the draft. But he went on to play nine seasons with the Giants and made five Pro Bowls. As a linebacker who could play all over the field, Armstead often led the team in tackles.

Amani Toomer proved to be an excellent returner. He returned a punt for a touchdown in his first game in 1996. By 1999, the Giants realized he would make an excellent receiver

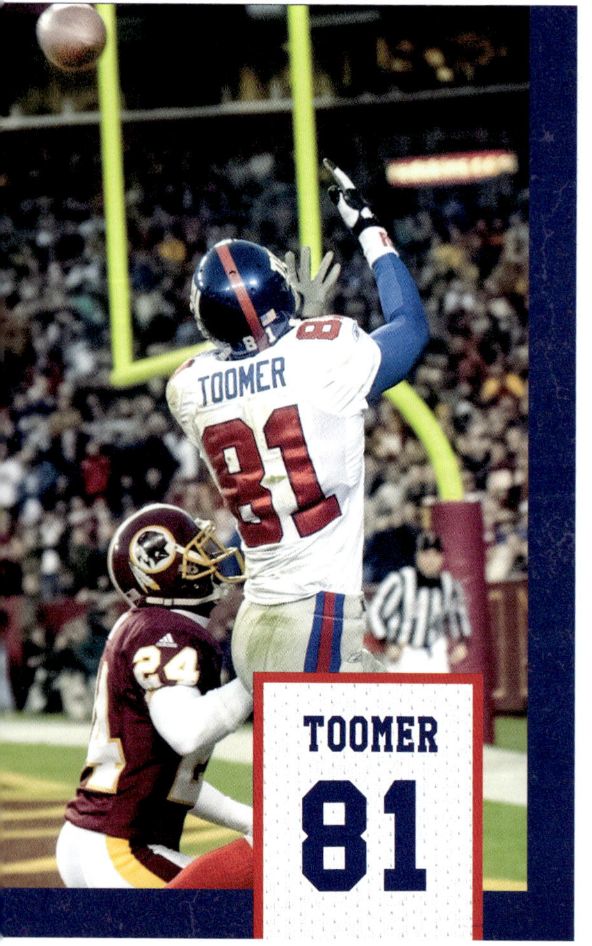

as well. Toomer wound up as the team's all-time leader in receptions, receiving yards, and receiving touchdowns.

Running back **Tiki Barber** joined Toomer on the Giants in 1997. He went on to become the team's greatest ever at his

position. Short but speedy, Barber racked up 10,449 yards in 10 seasons.

Quarterback **Eli Manning** came to the Giants in 2004 with massive expectations. The brother of NFL legend Peyton Manning mostly

STAT SPOTLIGHT

CAREER PASSING YARDS

GIANTS TEAM RECORD

Eli Manning: 57,023

lived up to them. He led the Giants to two Super Bowl titles and became the team's all-time leading passer. Manning was also durable. He started 210 games in a row at one point.

The Giants had never seen a rookie like **Saquon Barkley**. The running back set team rookie records in 2018 with 1,307 rushing yards and 11 touchdowns. Barkley also caught 91 passes. Like Frank Gifford decades earlier, he was another all-around offensive threat for Big Blue.

TOM COUGHLIN

Tom Coughlin won his first Super Bowl ring with the Giants in 1990. That was when he was an assistant. He won two more when he returned as head coach in 2004. That included beating the New England Patriots in Super Bowl XLII. The 2007 Patriots were undefeated going into the game. The Giants' victory was one of the biggest upsets in NFL history.

BARKLEY
26

TIMELINE

1925
STEVE OWEN
(1926–31, 1933)
1930
RAY FLAHERTY
(1928–29, 1931–35)
MEL HEIN
(1931–45)
1940
EMLEN TUNNELL
(1948–58)
KEN STRONG
(1933–35, 1939, 1944–47)
1950
FRANK GIFFORD
(1952–60, 1962–64)
CHARLIE CONERLY
(1948–61)
1960
ROSEY BROWN
(1953–65)
1970
HARRY CARSON
(1976–88)
PHIL SIMMS
(1979–93)
1980
CARL BANKS
(1984–92)
LAWRENCE TAYLOR
(1981–93)
1990
MICHAEL STRAHAN
(1993–2007)
JESSIE ARMSTEAD
(1993–2001)
2000
AMANI TOOMER
(1996–2008)
TIKI BARBER
(1997–2006)
2010
ELI MANNING
(2004–19)
SAQUON BARKLEY
(2018–)
2020

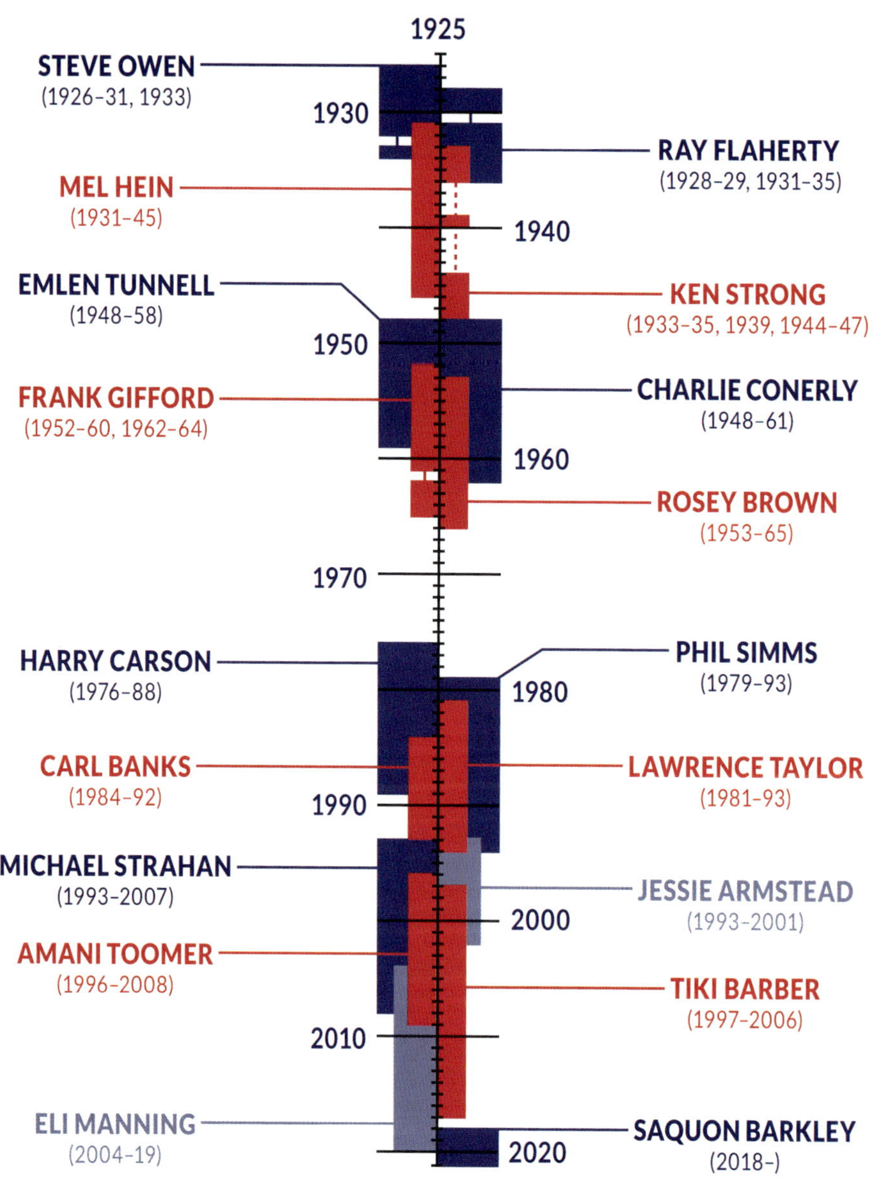

TEAM FACTS

NEW YORK GIANTS

Founded: 1925

NFL championships: 4 (1927, 1934, 1938, 1956)

Super Bowl titles: 4 (1986, 1990, 2007, 2011)*

Key coaches:

- **Steve Owen** (1930–53), 153–100–17, 2 NFL championships
- **Bill Parcells** (1983–90), 77–49–1, 2 Super Bowl titles
- **Tom Coughlin** (2004–15), 102–90–0, 2 Super Bowl titles

MORE INFORMATION

To learn more about the New York Giants, go to **pressboxbooks.com/AllAccess**.

These links are routinely monitored and updated to provide the most current information available.

**1966 through 2020*

GLOSSARY

coordinator
An assistant coach who is in charge of the offense, defense, or special teams.

draft
An event that allows teams to choose new players coming into the league.

franchise quarterback
A quarterback capable of leading a team for a number of years.

linebacker
A player who lines up behind the defensive linemen and in front of the defensive backs.

Pro Bowl
The NFL's all-star game, in which the league's best players compete.

reception
A forward pass that results in a catch.

routed
Defeated in a decisive way.

sack
A tackle of the quarterback behind the line of scrimmage.

INDEX